SO WHAT YOU'RE SCARED. GIRL, DO IT ANYWAY!

8 powerful
steps
to overcome
fear and begin
to live your
dreams

Sandra Denise Parker

Your Time's UP, Fear!

Copyright © 2025 by Sandra Denise Parker

All rights reserved.

No portion of this book may be reproduced in any form without written permission from the publisher or author, except as permitted by United States of America copyright law.

Photography: Slick Angles in Columbia SC

Makeup: Esthetized by Nadia LLC in Columbia SC

Dedication

This book is dedicated to all the women who grapple with fear, self-doubt, and limiting beliefs. These emotions can rob you of the freedom to embrace the life you truly deserve. I understand these struggles deeply, having endured them for years. While I may not have conquered all my fears, I have learned to navigate through them. Today, my life is a transformation from my past. I am actively pursuing my goals and realizing my dreams. Remember, you can achieve this too. This book is for you, and I can't wait to meet you on the other side of fear.

With all my love,

Queen

Table of Contents

Preface 1

Chapter 1
What is Fear? 9

Chapter 2
The Mysterious Presence of Fear 17

Chapter 3
Embracing
the Courage
to Acknowledge Your Fear 27

Chapter 4
Peeling Back the Layers and
Unveiling the Root Cause of Fear 33

Chapter 5
The Magic of Writing: The Power of the Pen 41

Chapter 6
The Trinity of Empowerment:
Prayer, Meditation, and Positive Affirmations 51

Chapter 7
Harnessing Wisdom: The Power of Knowledge 59

Chapter 8
Embracing the Dance of Baby Steps 69

Chapter 9
Paint Your Path to Success:
The Power of Visualization 77

Chapter 10
The Power of Influence:
Surround Yourself with Successful People. 87

Conclusion 95

About the Author 101

Preface

"The graveyard is the richest place on the earth, because it is here you will find all the hopes and dreams that were never fulfilled. The books that were never written, songs never sung, the inventions that were never shared, the cures that were never discovered. All because someone was too afraid to take that first step, keep with the problem, or determined to carry out their dream."

—Les Brown

Wow! Take a deep breath and let that sink in. The weight of unfulfilled dreams is heavy, isn't it? In "So What You're Scared Girl, Do It Anyway!" I invite you on a journey to gently unravel those fears and rediscover the power within you. Yes, you, my friend, are more powerful than you can ever imagine.

Now, you might be wondering why you should trust me. Allow me to introduce myself. I'm Sandra, affectionately known as Queen. This title was gifted to me by one of my favorite ER physicians who said I was a born leader and I carried myself very regally. Little did he know, in that moment I was grappling with some of the toughest challenges of my life. Isn't it magical how others can see a bright light within us when we can't even recognize it ourselves?

Today, I'm a free spirit, a solo-traveler enthusiast who's visited over 70 countries, embracing the joy of life and connecting with everyone around me. Having spent over 30 years as a Registered Nurse and 15 of these years in nurse leadership, my journey has been filled with nurturing, healing, mentoring, and coaching others. It's this path that led me to become a transformational life coach, motivational speaker, and author, specializing in leadership and the beautiful realm of self-love. I guide women to utilize the power they have within to release emotions of self-doubt, low self-esteem, and fear. Emotions that are keeping them from achieving their goals and dreams.

Preface

Every heart carries a dream or many. As a bedside nurse, I've been privileged to share countless intimate conversations with both the elderly and younger individuals facing chronic illnesses. So many of these discussions begin with a gentle sigh and the words, "I wish I had done this… I wish I had pursued that… If only I had more time." It's heartbreaking to see how fear, along with the weight of parental, societal and cultural expectations, hold so many people back from embracing their true desires. The fear of rejection or judgement can silence dreams that yearn to be realized. There is an old cliché that whispers, "Parents are often the silent killers of dreams."

This rings true when parents push their children to become doctors or lawyers, sometimes insisting on these paths because they themselves could never pursue such professions. These expectations often arise from cultural traditions, like being the fourth generation in a family of doctors. Meanwhile, the child's passion is to be a musician or an artist. It serves as a reminder that love can sometimes stretch its arms too tightly around aspirations, stifling the very life we were meant to live.

As a nurse leader and now a transformational life coach, I've witnessed countless dedicated and talented clients and colleagues hesitating to pursue advancement or achieve their goals due to the tangled web of excuses that stem from fear. It's disheartening to see these remarkable individuals, who have so much potential to shine, hold themselves back. The saddest part is that without someone to recognize and nurture their gifts, they risk drifting aimlessly, lost in the shadows. Their talent goes untapped, and the dreams they hold remain dormant, hidden from the world and even themselves. This serves as a gentle reminder: sometimes, all it takes is a little encouragement to help someone embrace their journey of self-discovery.

How can I be so certain about the words I speak? Because this is my truth. I once stood in the very shoes of those I speak about. I wasn't always this confident woman speaking to you today. My past was filled with self-doubt and anxiety. Many times, I needed encouragement from others to take the leaps of faith necessary to grasp the opportunities that came my way. Opportunities that would elevate and enhance my life and career. Growing up in the projects of Brooklyn, New York, was no easy task. Each day, I navigated a landscape filled with fear, struggling to break free from a "crab in a barrel" society where being different often meant facing harsh consequences. Can you relate to feeling trapped in a world that demands conformity, where family, culture, and societal rules stifle your true self?

Adding another layer to my struggles, I endured the trauma of a sexual assault from a family friend at the age of fourteen. Shame, fear, and guilt kept me silent for many years. Later in my young adult life, I found myself in a physically and mentally abusive relationship, which only deepened these feelings. I found myself overwhelmed and paralyzed by procrastination. I was a people pleaser, suffocated by imposter syndrome, terrified of the possibility of failure, or even success. I knew how to survive in the concrete jungle. It was instinctual. Could I survive outside of it was the question that scared me. Yet my desire to escape the chains of my circumstances and not become just another statistic burned brighter than my fear. Thank God for that resilience.

Today, thoughts of fear may pop up from time to time, but I've learned how to overcome them and move forward. The eight powerful steps, detailed in the chapters that follow, are what helped me work through my fear and I continue to use them everyday. I'm so eager to share them with you.

First, let me share with you how I even formulated these steps. One day, as I sat quietly reflecting on my life and the challenges I had faced, I began to think about what I did to make it through those tough times. That's when the light bulb turned on. I realized that the steps I took were simple and straightforward, yet incredibly powerful. All that time, I had made life so complicated, trying to navigate challenges with unnecessary complexity. It's like trying to solve a puzzle without realizing that sometimes the simplest piece is what completes the picture. If these practices helped me, why not share them? I realized my insights could empower others, offering them a roadmap to navigate their own fears. And that's how these eight powerful transformative steps came to life.

Utilizing these tools have helped me become profoundly at peace with myself, loving this amazing woman I have become. I am still growing, taking immense pride in my many accomplishments, especially my willingness to share my journey with others.

It takes courage to expose our vulnerabilities. Often, we wish for our past to remain hidden, allowing the world to see only our new and improved selves. But I firmly believe that it would be unfair because, in doing so, we deny others the chance to find solace in our shared experiences. People need to know they aren't alone in their hardships, that they aren't the only ones who've made mistakes and struggled in this thing called life. By sharing our journeys, we extend a helping hand to those going through similar challenges, showing them that there is a way to overcome, to transform, and to embrace the strength that lies within.

So, here is my why behind writing this book. Are you ready to take this incredible journey with me, Beautiful Queen? Together we're going to conquer our fears, achieve our goals, and turn those dreams into reality.

So, what you're scared? Girl, do it anyway!

Love you!

Queen

Chapter 1

What is Fear?

"The fears we cannot conquer become barriers to our happiness."

—Karen Salmansohn

HELLO, BEAUTIFUL QUEEN! I AM so excited. Before we dive into this chapter, let me share something important: I wrote this book for *you*. To empower you, inspire you, and guide you on your journey, So, please grab your pen and highlighter! Mark the passages that resonate, because you'll want to revisit them later. Remember, the first step to overcoming any challenge is acknowledging its presence. Let's dig deep and explore these effective strategies for conquering fear, empowering you to fulfill your life-long goals and embrace the life you truly deserve.

Before we can get into how to overcome fear, we need to define it. Fear is a complex and universal emotion that plays a significant role in our lives. It can be both a protective mechanism and a hinderance. Fear is that unpleasant feeling that creeps up on us when we believe that something or someone is dangerous or could cause us pain. It's a natural emotion that we all experience at some point in our lives. And you know what? In many cases, fear is a good thing. It's our body's way of protecting us from harm. Like when we instinctively jump back from a snake or scary insect. Or when we hear a loud noise and automatically run in the opposite direction.

However, fear can be a tricky little devil. It can influence our thoughts and actions, holding us back from truly living our lives to the fullest. It can stop us from enjoying the things that bring us joy, from living our best life, from leaving unhealthy situations, or from taking risks and pursuing our dreams. There was a time when I allowed myself to be stuck in a cycle of comfort and familiarity, even though I knew deep down I was meant for something greater. That's not a good place to be in, my friend. You see, I stayed in an abusive relationship far too long, because I feared not being able to provide for myself and my daughter. Sometimes we let our fears control our present and stop us from stepping into a beautiful future.

Question: Have you ever found yourself trapped in an unhealthy situation, allowing fear to hold you back from seeking positive change? Maybe you were so accustomed to the familiar discomfort that the thought of stepping into the unknown was scary and overwhelming. This happens often, not just in our personal lives but also in our professional lives. Have you ever stayed at a job that you disliked because you were afraid to look for a new one? You've been there long enough that you have become comfortable with being unhappy. Maybe you are like I used to be; the fear of failure keeps you from moving up the career ladder, so you stay stagnant, knowing you are clearly qualified for a better position.

The great thing is we have the power to control fear. Yes, you heard me right, we can take charge of our fears and not let them dictate our lives. It all starts with acknowledging our fears, shining a light on them, and understanding where they come from. You see, fear often stems from past experiences, traumas, or limiting beliefs that we've picked up along the way and when we can identify those underlying causes, we can begin the process of healing and releasing those fears.

Now, I'm not saying it's easy. Confronting our fears can be downright scary itself, but remember, fear is just an emotion. Just like guilt, shame, anger, joy, happiness, and sadness. It's not a permanent state of being and just like all the other emotions we feel, we can control them, and so we can control fear as well. We have the power within us to overcome it. It's about tapping into our inner strength, our resilience, and belief in ourselves.

So, how do we do it? It all starts with shifting our mindset. Instead of seeing fear as something to run away from, we must choose to see it as an opportunity for growth and our transformation. We must look at our fears as challenges to overcome, steppingstones on our path to success. It's about embracing the discomfort and uncertainty that comes with facing our fears head-on.

Let me tell you beautiful Queen, never be ashamed of being fearful. You are not alone in this journey. We all have fears, even the most successful and confident women. Fear is a natural part of the journey, especially for women stepping into greatness. Here are a few examples:

- **Oprah Winfrey:** Once terrified of public speaking, Oprah confronted her fear and became a media mogul, inspiring millions!

- **J.K Rowling:** Battled extreme self-doubt and rejection. She was a single mother surviving on government assistance before Harry Potter became a global phenomenon. She didn't let fear hold her back.

- **Beyoncé:** Her stage fright pushed her to invent an alter ego, "Sasha Fierce," to help deal with it. Today she is the one of the top female entertainers in the world.

- **Meryl Streep:** One of my favorite actresses had crippling anxiety before auditioning for roles. She learned how to channel that fear into passionate performances. I'm so happy she did because what would I do without *The Devil Wears Prada*?

The key is to step into your fear. Turn your fear into your fuel and remember that it is temporary, just like any other emotion. Surround yourself with a support system of like-minded people who can uplift and encourage you along the way. Seek out mentors or coaches or friends who have faced their own fears and came out stronger on the other side.

Their stories and guidance can be invaluable as you navigate your own fears.

Remember, healing from fear takes time. It's a process. It's important to be kind and patient to yourself along the way. Celebrate every small step you take, no matter how big or small. Most importantly, don't be afraid to ask for help when you need it. Asking for help is not a weakness. It is a strength. Seeking professional support, such as therapy or counseling, can provide you with the tools and strategies to overcome your fears and live a more fulfilling life.

So, Queen, it's time to take control of your fears by acknowledging them and understanding where they come from. Only after doing this will you be able to shift your mindset to see them as opportunities for growth. Surround yourself with a supportive community and be gentle with yourself as you navigate this journey. You have the power within you to overcome any fear that stands in your way. Believe in yourself and watch as you unleash your true potential. Fear may have been holding you back, but now it's time to step into your power and live the life you were meant to live.

Stay tuned, Queen. Now that we have defined what fear is, in the next pages we'll be talking about how fear may be unknowingly showing up in your life.

Chapter 2

The Mysterious Presence of Fear

"Nothing in life is to be feared. It is only to be understood. Now is the time to understand more, so that we may fear less."

—Marie Curie

IN THIS CHAPTER WE WILL discover the many ways fear may unknowingly show up in your life. It can show up in many ways you least expect. Fear has many characteristics. It's not always sweaty palms, shaky knees, and heart palpitations. Fear can be hidden in our reactions to situations. For instance, I was once a perfectionist, queen of excuses, and a procrastinator. I had so many projects that were never completed. They were amazing too. However, I thought maybe if I change this and add that it would be better. I would put it to the side and start on another brilliant idea without completing the last one. I was cheating the world from my creations. Once I understood that nothing is perfect, I started making huge progress. I was able to complete my projects and share them with others. To see the joy that some of those items brought to others made my heart fill with joy and pride. Queens, done is better than perfect! I need you to understand the power of this statement.

I realized these characteristics stemmed from fear. Read on to discover how fear may have a mysterious presence in your life.

Did you know micromanaging has a very deep connection to fear? You see, micromanaging often stems from a place of insecurity, and fear of the unknown. It's that protective shield that you put up to ensure that everything goes exactly as planned, leaving no room for errors or surprises. The fear of failure drives micromanaging. You may worry that if you don't have complete control over every little detail, things will go wrong and reflect poorly on you. Perfectionism at its finest. This fear can be paralyzing, but Queen, it's important to remember that failure is a natural part of growth and learning. By allowing others freedom to make their own decisions, and learn from their own mistakes, you create an environment that fosters growth and innovation.

The fear of losing control is another fuel for micromanaging. You may feel that if you loosen your grip and trust others to take charge, things will spin out of control. However, Queen, you are a leader, whether you're at home or in the office. You are the CEO of your kingdom and true leaders are about empowering others and creating a sense of trust and collaboration.

So, why not consider allowing little Michael or Madeliene to have more responsibilities around the house? By assigning them daily or weekly tasks, you can help them develop independence and a sense of responsibility.

Similarly, why not let John take the lead on that project at the office, with you serving as his resource person? This will not only make him feel trusted and valued, but it will also free up some time for yourself. In both instances you will be able to focus on completing tasks that only you can handle. By delegating and trusting others, you'll not only empower them but also create more space for yourself to accomplish what truly requires your attention.

Being perceived as incompetent is another area of fear that drives micromanaging. You may feel the need to constantly prove yourself and demonstrate to others that you are the expert by being involved in every little detail. I like to call it "marking my territory." This fear is often about the worry that others see you as inadequate and can stem from a lack of confidence in yourself. Remember, every expert was once a beginner. It is important to recognize that true competence lies in your ability to lead and inspire others, not in your ability to control every aspect of your life or projects. When you empower others and trust in their abilities, you create a team that thrives and achieves great accomplishments together at home and in business.

There is a very famous African proverb that states: "If you want to go fast, go alone, if you want to go far, go together."

Fear of failure is one of the main reasons people procrastinate and become stagnant. When we are faced with a task that feels challenging or unfamiliar, fear can creep in, causing you to put off starting or completing your project. The fear of rejection, criticism, failure, you name it, caused me to take five years to write my first book, ***On My Own: A Guide to Finding Yourself Through Female Solo Travel***. I was such a perfectionist that it led to frustration, which led to procrastination. On top of that I became fearful of success. "Oh my God, what if this book becomes a number-one bestseller, will I ever be able to top it?" I started doubting my own abilities, thinking I wouldn't be able to replicate success. I had to stop panicking over things that hadn't even happened yet and start taking massive action. So, I hired a publishing company to help me get to the finish line. What took me five years on my own only took me six months with them. It was a great decision, one I will never regret.

Let's talk about paralysis. Fear can paralyze you. You know exactly what you should do, but fear takes over and you freeze. Instead of doing something, any little thing, you do nothing at all. It is self-sabotage at its finest. You're so scared of the uncertainty that you sabotage your own success by not doing anything or taking opportunities. You avoid taking risks, even though everything you want is on the other side of that fear. Breaking through that fear and embracing the unknown is when you truly begin to live.

Another characteristic of fear is the endless excuses we create. When fear takes hold, it conjures up a myriad of reasons why we can't pursue our dreams: "It's not the right time" or "I don't know what to do." This fear of failure, rejection, and criticism floods our minds, leading to self-doubt that ultimately sabotages our efforts. Instead of facing our fears, we often find someone or something to blame for our inaction.

It's time to kick those excuses to the curb and start believing in ourselves. Remember, the desires nestled in your heart are already a part of who you are, just waiting for the moment you decide to nurture them into existence. I firmly believe that if you dream of something or feel a desire to create, it's because you possess the power within you to make it a reality. Everything you need to unleash your incredible potential is already deep within your beautiful soul. Embrace the magic within you, Queen, and watch your dreams come to life when you take decisive action.

Now, let's dive into the impact of losing your voice. When fear grips you, it can silence your inner strength, leaving you hesitant to speak up for yourself. The worries of judgement, retaliation, and ridicule, loom large, making you fear disappointing others and straining relationships. In the process, you become a people pleaser, constantly prioritizing everyone else's needs while sidelining your own. You find yourself saying "yes" to demands, even when your gut is screaming "no." Your decision making is based off the opinions of others. This reliance on external validation becomes your compass. When there is no validation, there is no action, and your dreams remain on hold.

Let me tell you from experience—people pleasing is utterly exhausting, and it leaves you feeling empty because you're living your life for everyone else. Telling someone "no" terrified me. My stomach would tie up in knots, and guilt would wash over me when I felt I couldn't accommodate their requests. I would scramble to find a way to make it happen, meanwhile, my own goals, dreams, and projects were left unattended, and I found myself feeling unfulfilled. And here's a little kicker—can you guess?—those very same people never had a problem saying "no" to me when I needed help with something.

So, Queen it's time to reclaim your voice and live authentically! The world craves the real you and the unique gifts only you can offer, whether it's baking exquisite cakes, designing stunning dresses or anything else that lights you up. Your value is immeasurable, yet you may never come to realize it if you continue to let fear dictate your journey.

Now, I need you to understand that fear isn't just a mental struggle. It can manifest physically, too. Living in a constant state of worry and people pleasing can drain your energy, mess with your sleep, and even lead to unwanted weight loss or gain. Chronic stress fueled by fear puts you at risk for a whole host of diseases and health conditions, from heart attacks and high blood pressure to diabetes and gastrointestinal problems. You name it. It's a heavy toll to bear.

Lastly, fear can cause negative coping mechanisms. When it takes hold, unhealthy habits may creep in, manifesting as depression, anxiety, frustration, and a deep sense of hopelessness. It's all too easy to resort to substances, turning to drugs, prescription medications, alcohol, cigarettes, or even overeating to numb the distress that fear brings. If you find yourself in this place, please seek professional help. It is time to embrace healthier ways to confront and express your emotions.

Can you see yourself in any of these characteristics? If so, don't worry. I invite you to keep reading because I have **eight powerful steps** waiting for you, ready to inspire and empower you on your journey to fearlessness. Together, we'll uncover the **first step** to reclaiming your strength over fear in the next chapter.

Remember if you need to take a break, that's okay. Just don't stay away too long. Knowledge is your greatest ally, and the road to freedom begins with decisive action. I'll be waiting for you on the next page.

Chapter 3

Embracing the Courage to Acknowledge Your Fear

"The key to growth is acknowledging your fear of the unknown and jumping in anyway"

—Jen Sincero

IN THIS CHAPTER, WE'RE GOING to dive deep into the power of acknowledging your fear. This is **the first powerful step** to breaking free from the chains of fear. It's time to face it head-on, my friend, and take control of your life. So, grab a cup of tea or coffee, find a cozy spot, and let's get real about fear. Remember, the first step is always the hardest, but it is crucial. The only way we can resolve our issue is by acknowledging that there is one.

As I previously stated, fear is a powerful emotion that can grip us tightly and hold us back from reaching our potential. It can paralyze us, leaving us feeling stuck and unable to move forward. I know this feeling all too well, as I've experienced it myself on many times. One memory that stands out vividly happened when I was just thirteen years old.

Every Saturday at two p.m. I would attend youth choir practice at Wayside Baptist Church in Brooklyn, New York. The church was a beautifully renovated two-story movie theater, adorned with ornate gold decor on the walls, large Greek marble columns, and plush burgundy carpet lining the four aisles. The church had a regal feel to it.

As a member of the choir, I loved the feeling of singing with my family and fellow choir members. However, there was one thing that always terrified me—being in the spotlight. This Saturday started off no different than the others. I walked down the aisle and sang out loud as I strolled, marveling at the astonishing acoustics of the church. I loved singing, but deep down I was afraid of being chosen to lead a song or perform a solo. I would always hope and pray that I wouldn't be called upon and I didn't know why, since God gifted me with a beautiful voice.

I took my regular seat in the soprano section—third pew, fourth seat to the left. Once everyone arrived, the choir director began to play a new song, "It Is Well with My Soul" by Horatio Spafford. It's an old gospel hymn but was new to this choir. The choir director looked over her glasses, as she usually did when she was trying to decide who would lead. She took a brief look into the tenor section, then shifted her gaze to the alto section, before quickly focusing on the soprano section. I said to myself, "Lord, please don't let her pick me." I could feel my heart racing and my palms becoming sweaty. I tried to shrink into my seat, hoping to miraculously disappear, but fear had other plans for me. I closed my eyes tight and then it happened. She called my name. In that moment, I felt the wave of panic wash over me. I tried to respond, but my voice failed. I attempted to stand up, but it felt as if my body was frozen in place. Fear had taken complete control.

It was in that moment I truly felt the power of fear and how it was negatively impacting my life. I said to myself, "What is this thing that has control over me like this?" I realized it was stage fright. I acknowledged my fear, and I gave my fear a name. It was no longer an abstract concept; it was very real, and I didn't know if I could overcome it.

Now, I want to ask you, have you ever experienced a similar situation where fear paralyzed you? Perhaps it was a fear of public speaking, heights or even something as simple as making a dreaded phone call. Take a moment to reflect on that experience and how it made you feel. Did you acknowledge and identify your fear?

Acknowledging and identifying our fears is the first step towards conquering them. It's about shining a light on the darkness and bringing our fears to the open. By giving our fears a name, we take back some of the power.

My choir director truly understood the depths of my stage fright. Recognizing the unique challenges I faced as the pastor's niece, coming from a lineage of exceptionally talented singers in my family, only added to the pressure I felt. The thought of being criticized and judged by the church members had me shaking. What was worse, the thought of being ridiculed by my family if my singing fell short. *That* terrified me.

Thankfully, there was a solution to this problem if I was willing to act. My choir director graciously opened her home to provide me with private sessions. She gave me support and guidance. So did her family. They were my audience. I gradually built up the courage to face my fear head-on, and when the moment came for me to sing my debut, I was still nervous, but I felt a newfound sense of preparedness. I was so happy. The performance turned out to be amazing. Yes! I beat fear at its game.

This experience opened more doors for me later. I would be asked to sing at weddings and other social functions. Did you notice I said I still felt fearful? But I did it anyway! The difference was I was more prepared. Action comes first, then confidence follows. The more I sang lead, the more confident I became. I was still nervous before each performance, but I'd learned how to work through it.

Once we acknowledge our fears, we can begin the journey of overcoming them. When you acknowledge your fear, you are taking a brave step towards self-awareness and empowerment. It's about recognizing that fear is a natural part of the human experience, but not allowing it to control or limit you. Confronting your fears is not easy, my friend, but it's necessary if we want to live a life free from the constraints of fear. Remind yourself of what you want—that desire is on the other side of your fear. Seek support from professionals, mentors, or a community who can guide you through the process. Remember, you are not on this journey alone.

As you embark on this journey of conquering your fears, I encourage you to acknowledge them with boldness and determination. Embrace this journey as an opportunity for transformation and growth. Just like I confronted my stage fright, you can confront your fear head-on as well. You have the power within to conquer fear and create a life that is filled with joy, purpose, and abundance. You are capable of so much more than you can even imagine. Embrace the journey. Transform your fear into fuel for your dreams. You've got this!

Now might be a good time to stretch or get a cup of tea or coffee. Don't go away too far…. In the next chapter we are going to learn to peel back the layers and unveil the root cause of our fear.

Chapter 4

Peeling Back the Layers and Unveiling the Root Cause of Fear

"There seem to be endless obstacles… It seemed that the root cause of them all was fear."

—Marion Miller

Welcome back, beautiful Queen. In this chapter, we are going to dig deep and talk about how to unmask the sneaky culprit behind your fear. Identifying the root cause of fear is **the second power-**

ful step to breaking free from fear's chains. Fear can come from all sorts of places, such as traumatic experiences and negative self-talk. It can even stem from the contagious fear of those around us. It's like we absorb fear through osmosis just because someone close to us is afraid of something. We start trembling in our boots too. I want to share a little story with you from my life that will have you laughing and gasping and maybe even nodding your head in recognition. Get ready for an exhilarating ride filled with laughter and insight from my own self-discovery.

Picture this: my mother had a fear of driving on big parkways and over bridges. Now, I don't know about you, but as a kid, six or seven years old, I found that perplexing. Even at that age, I loved architecture, and it fascinated me how these large pieces of steel suspended over a river could hold so many cars and trucks at one time without caving in. It made me curious, but it terrified my mom. I mean, bridges are architectural wonders and the views driving across are often beautiful. But there my mom was, lying down in the backseat of the car whenever my father drove us across the Verrazano Bridge from Brooklyn to New Jersey. My mother never drove over a bridge, but whenever she had to drive on the parkway, she was in the slow lane doing thirty miles per hour gripping that steering wheel for dear life.

Fast forward to when I finally got my driver's license. Guess what? I became terrified of driving over bridges and on large parkways. Can you believe it? Me, the girl who was fascinated by the intricate designs and breathtaking views suddenly had a tight chest and a constricted throat, whenever I approached a bridge or a parkway. It was like my body was playing a cruel joke on me. Did I inherit my mothers fears?

Hold on friends, because here comes the plot twist! I want you to imagine another scene: it's a beautiful spring evening, and I'm happily living with my boyfriend. We were supposed to go out to dinner, but he had to take a business client out instead. He asked if we could postpone our date until tomorrow. He was usually a man of his word so I was okay with it. And then, out of the blue, I accidentally overhear a conversation coming from our bedroom that spills the beans on his not-so-innocent plans with another woman. "Are you kidding me?" I muttered to myself, trying not to laugh from astonishment. Reminder, this was in the early eighties, the time of landlines and pagers. So, I snuck into the kitchen like a ninja spy to pick up the telephone and eavesdrop on their chat. And what do I hear? She is telling him she wants to ride in his fancy sports car. Seriously, you can't make this stuff up! My heart sank, but there was no time for tears and drama because I'm no drama queen. So, quick thinking kicks in. I was already dressed to the nines, believing he'd be taking me out. I hatched a sneaky escape plan. Off I went, tiptoeing outside, and guess what ride I took? His 1979 pristine white Corvette Stingray with red leather bucket seats and a cool T-top. She might have secured a rendezvous with him, but on that night, under those stars, she would not experience the thrill of riding in that car. Period!

Now, try not to judge me, I want you to think back and remember a time when you did something completely out of character or out of desperation over a relationship. It hurt like hell then, but today you can laugh about it. I'm sitting here laughing with you just imagining what you did. I know you did something wild, because looking back I can't believe some of the things I've done. We all know that love and pride will make you do some crazy and dumb things. Okay, back to the story.

I had to think fast about where to go. I couldn't stay local because he would find me. Okay, I thought, I'll go to New Jersey to my aunt's house. I was pulling out of the driveway when I saw him running trying to stop me. Too late! I was filled with laughter and as I sped down the main street my heart was racing. I couldn't believe I got away. As I made it to the Belt Parkway heading towards Verrazano Bridge, something magical happened. I realized that I wasn't afraid of driving. I was enjoying the drive. I had the music blasting too—ironically, Michael Jackson's "Wanna Be Startin' Somethin'" was playing on the radio. The sky was so beautiful, the stars were out. My boyfriend had left the T-top open in preparation for his date. That Corvette was hugging the ground and driving as smooth as butter.

It was at that moment I realized it was all a sham. I did not inherit my mother's fear of driving on parkways and over bridges. This wasn't a biological inherited problem like high blood pressure or diabetes. However, I had allowed the memories of my mother's fear to seep into my own psyche. I'd let it handicap me from experiencing the freedom and joy of driving without fear. Did I blame her?

Of course not, but it sure felt good to be free from those chains of fear.

As I looked down at the speedometer, a hilarious thought popped into my head: *What if I get a ticket? I'm doing ninety miles per hour.* But then another thought came: *Oh, my goodness, what if he reported this car stolen?* Now that was fearful. Imagine me, Queen, all dolled up and ready to slay, being caught in a prison photo with handcuffs and an orange jumpsuit. Can you picture that? The thought was horrific. So, I slowed down, and I prayed to God all the way back home from New Jersey that I would make it without the police pulling me over. I did make it back safe and sound. And guess what? My boyfriend wasn't even home when I got there. He took the heifer out in the Cadillac smelling of cologne and wore an outfit that I had bought him. I was too tired to be pissed! I took a shower and went to bed.

I learned some very valuable lessons that night. One of them being, no man is worth all of that. The second one was that I deserved better. Self-love and relationships are a whole book by itself. I think my next book will be about that. I've got some real good stories and valuable lessons to share. However, analyzing the root cause of my fear was the most valuable lesson of all. I've been driving on parkways and over bridges ever since.

Identifying the root cause of your fear is not always easy. It's a very transformative process. It may require delving into past traumas, examining negative self-talk, and challenging limiting beliefs, but it is a necessary step towards healing and growth. By understanding where your fear originated, you can begin to dismantle its hold on your life. For some, it could be a childhood incident, a failed relationship, or a professional setback. These experiences can leave us with deep emotional scars, shaping our perspectives on the world and instilling a sense of fear and vulnerability. We may often internalize the criticisms and judgements of others, creating a negative narrative that holds us back from pursuing our dreams. It's important to change these beliefs and replace them with empowering thoughts and affirmations.

In some cases, fear may be absorbed from those around us, just like I absorbed my mother's fear. We are social beings, and we often pick up on the fears and anxieties of our loved ones and friends. It's important to recognize when we are carrying someone else's fear and consciously choose to release it. We must remember that fear is not our birthright; it is a learned response that can be unlearned.

Analyzing the root cause of your fear is a deeply personal journey. It requires courage. It requires you to be vulnerable and committed to self-discovery, but I promise you that the rewards are immeasurable. By understanding the origins of your fear, you can begin to rewrite your story and reclaim your power.

So, take a moment to reflect on your own fears. What are the root causes? Is it past trauma, negative self-talk, or fear absorbed from others? Write it down, explore it, and allow yourself to feel the emotions that arise. Remember, this is a process of healing and growth, and it may take time.

Remember, also, to be gentle and kind to yourself. This journey is not about blaming or shaming anyone. It's about understanding and releasing. If you get stuck in this area, seek support from professionals, mentors, or a community who can guide you through the process. There is nothing wrong with asking for help. You do not have to be alone on this journey. I'll see you in the next chapter.

Chapter 5

The Magic of Writing: The Power of the Pen

"Writing in a journal gives me a place to report, interpret, save, question, predict, unload, praise, compare, cry, laugh, draw, paint and remember"

—Luci Swindoll

OKAY, BEAUTIFUL QUEEN. LET'S TALK about the magic of journaling and how it can help you dance with fear and move forward fearlessly. This is **the third powerful step** to breaking free from fear's chains. The power of the pen is amazing! When you hold one in your hand, you control the narrative. I refer to it as a royal scepter. A visual representation of a ruler's authority and power giving you, Queen, the power to write your life story. You get to decide how it ends.

Once you start pouring your heart onto those pages, you're creating a sacred space for self-discovery and growth. I describe journaling as having a soul-to-soul conversation with myself. Trust me and give it a try because this is where the magic begins. It's within this intimate dialogue that fear starts to loosen its grip on your heart and mind. With every stroke of your royal scepter, you gain clarity and perspective. You start to see fear not as an unconquerable force, but rather as a challenge to be faced. Writing helps you to break down these fears into manageable pieces, making them less scary and more approachable.

Now, I'm that lady that loves to tell a story as a reference. So let me tell you my story of how paper and ink became the whispers of my heart. It was during my first marriage, when I was a newlywed and young mother yet far from the warmth of home, family, and friends. In those moments of solitude journaling became my best friend and confidante. I spilled my soul onto those pages. The good, the bad, and all the challenges I was facing at the time. It really became my lifeline when life threw me a curve ball that socked me dead in the center of my chest. My heart. Can you believe it? Just a little over a year into marriage, I discovered my husband had betrayed my trust. He was having an affair with another woman. Yes, I had gotten out of a relationship with a cheater only to fall in love with and marry another one. The shock, heartache, humiliation, and devastation were all captured in the pages of my journal, pages filled with tear-drop stains. Eventually these pages would be filled with my plans to leave and my goals for the future. My journal held my hand through it all and never whispered a word to anyone.

Fast forward years later. Divorced with two children, I opened my heart to love again. However, my second marriage was a chapter filled with twists and turns like a crazy rollercoaster ride. The kind where two carts starts side by side, sharing a track before dramatically veering off in different directions. They seem to cross paths intermittently, but it's just an illusion, a mere fleeting moment of connection. I know what you're saying to yourself. "Boy, she really knows how to pick them!" It's called lack of self-love. Well anyway, my husband and I rode this rollercoaster for years. We'd separate and reconnect. It became like a dance, one that many couples can resonate with. We went to counseling hoping to reignite the sparks of magic. It worked for a while but soon fizzled away again. We were two birds singing different tunes, a couple reading from different books of different genres. Yet I stayed, and all the time the question dancing in my mind was: *Why Sandra, why?*

So, Queen, fear and its cunning self played its part in leading me to this marriage. And once I was there, fear continued to hold me captive, whispering lies that kept me from breaking free. Didn't I mention before how sly and conniving fear can truly be?

Journaling helped me understand that fear was quite the common companion on this journey. The whispers of doubt. The fear of another failed chapter of my life, the fear of the criticism from family and friends that come with it. There was the fear of loneliness. I was older now. Who was going to want me? A twice-divorced mother with two children. It was the fear of releasing the cozy familiarity we shared. The title of "wife" held a certain power and warmth, didn't it? So, I thought. It was a piece of my identity, a role I had grown accustomed to. Then there were the children. We had a beautiful, blended family. I didn't want to hurt or lose my relationship with my beautiful bonus children. Heck, I didn't want to hurt him either. He was not a villain. He just wasn't my heart's truest match, and I wasn't the yin to his yang.

Can you imagine the weight of the load I was carrying? As women, we sometimes find ourselves entangled in relationships for all the wrong reasons. Despite these relationships draining our essence, robbing us of our true selves and our sacred feminine energy, we stay. We fear causing pain to others, yet the one suffering the most is none other than ourselves.

Have you ever found yourself in a similar predicament? A situation where you had to make a choice that not only affected your own life, but also the lives of those around you? Regardless of your decision, someone was bound to experience hurt or disappointment.

Through the art of journaling, I embarked on a journey of self-discovery. I was able to peel back the layers of fear and apprehension. Most of all, I was able to analyze how I got into this situation in the first place. The red flags are always there. We simply choose to ignore them, hoping things will change or that we can make them change.

Journaling helped me to reflect on those moments. I realized there were no gentle reminders that told me to slow down or proceed with caution. Instead, there were unmistakable stop signs and glaring red flashing lights from the start. The last one being that I'd felt like I was a part of a somber funeral procession on the way to my wedding. It was the longest drive in history. What should have been one of the happiest days of my life felt like my worst. However, the fear of potential embarrassment had taken root too deeply within me. Instead of having the courage to turn around, I let fear win, and I found myself carrying out the duty of saying "I do."

Through journaling I discovered I was losing myself because I had not been true to myself or him. The truth was when I met him, I was afraid and tired of being alone. So, I married the first man who was kind to me. He told me the things I wanted and needed to hear. I didn't allow myself enough time to collect the data that dating is for. Regardless, the façade was costing me the most important person in my life. Me. I was losing my peace trying to be his. It was too high a price to pay for the sake of a love that wasn't aligned. Every word I wrote in my journal helped me to realize I wasn't moving towards my own goals and dreams; I was moving a step closer to breaking free from the fear that was keeping me there. A step toward a love that was unconditional, a love that started within myself. It wasn't just about ending the marriage. I was no longer afraid to be alone. I was reclaiming my own power, my own identity, and my own essence. Only *you* can give you that. No one else.

When you face times of uncertainty or anxiety, your journal serves as a grounding anchor. It's a safe space to explore your emotions honestly. When you let your feelings flow freely, you give yourself permission to process and heal. This allows you to create space for growth and transformation. As you journal more, you will find that your fears start to lose their intensity. They may not vanish completely, but fear's power will begin to diminish. You learn how to work through fear. Your confidence grows until you begin to know you have the strength to overcome it.

Queen, there is so much more magic that journaling can bring into your life as you courageously face your fears. Let's talk about it:

- **Empowerment and Ownership:** When you take the time to write about your fears, you are taking ownership of them. You acknowledge their presence, but you don't allow them to take control of your life. "So what, I'm afraid? I'm going to do it anyway."

- **Reducing Stress:** Journaling is very relaxing. It helps to calm and soothe you emotionally, reducing anxiety and stress.

- **Problem Solver:** As you journal you will discover that your mind will start to come up with solutions and strategies to your challenges. It's much easier to come up with solutions when you write them externally versus just thinking about them internally.

- **Builds Awareness:** Writing down your fears helps you become aware of the specific triggers and situations that provoke them. This awareness will help you learn not to react in the heat of the moment, but to take time to gain control over your emotions. This in turn will enable you to respond more effectively to your fears.

- **Unlock Your Creativity:** Journaling allows you to express your thoughts and emotions in many ways. Use it as your canvas for self-expression.

Write poems or a song. Draw art expressing how you are feeling about your fears. You may even discover a new career or a part-time hobby from it.

- **Track Your Progress:** Journaling allows you to see how far you've come. When you look back at earlier entries, you'll be amazed at the progress you've made. This will boost your confidence in your ability to tackle further challenges with fear.

- **Celebrating Self-Growth:** Whenever you conquer a fear or push through a challenging situation, your journal is a testament to your growth. It helps to see your strength, your power, and your capabilities during times of doubt. Don't forget to celebrate every win. No matter how big or small. Do something special for yourself. Celebrate you!

So, my Queen, pick up your journal and your royal scepter. Let the ink flow. Let journaling be your faithful companion on this journey of self-discovery and fear-conquering. Write about your fears, your worries, your doubts and watch as they shrink and fade. Your pen is not just a symbol of power, but a conduit of healing. Use it to rewrite your story, to claim your strength, and to step into a brighter, more fearless future.

Embrace the process with love and patience, knowing that you have a powerful ally to guide you. Watch as you blossom into the extraordinary person you are. A powerful and fearless Queen stepping into your brilliance and unleashing your full potential.

Remember, you got this, and I am cheering you on! Keep going, Queen. Next, we'll talk about my secret and favorite weapon: "The Trinity of Empowerment."

Chapter 6

The Trinity of Empowerment:
Prayer, Meditation, and Positive Affirmations

"Sometimes you have to say a little prayer and trust in something greater than you."

—author unknown

IN THIS CHAPTER, WE ARE diving deep into a topic that resonates very deeply with me. The incredible journey of fostering harmony with prayer, meditation, and positive affirmations. When fear comes knocking at your door, this is **the fourth power-**

ful step to breaking free from its chain. It is also my favorite. So, get comfortable, get ready for a cup of inspiration, and explore how these precious and powerful practices can help you work through your fears.

I want to start off by saying I'm not here to impose my beliefs on others. I'm simply sharing what has helped me on my journey to overcoming fear. In moments of turmoil, what brings me peace amidst the storm is my faith in a higher power, and I make no apologies for this. I refer to my higher power—God—for guidance and consultation in every aspect of my life. I believe embracing something greater than ourselves is invaluable.

Through my many travels around the world, I have come to understand that this higher power may take on a different form for different people. Whether you call it the Universe, Buddha, Jesus Christ, Ancestors, or another name that resonates with you, what matters is the connection you cultivate. My connection with God has been my lifeline during dark moments, helping me navigate fear while keeping me aligned, focused, and true to myself on a day-to-day basis.

I affectionately refer to this powerful combination of prayer, meditation, and positive affirmations as my "Trinity of Empowerment." It's a trio of actions that not only empowers me to face my fears but also fosters a profound sense of inner peace. When I take the time to pray, meditate, and affirm my strengths, I create a sanctuary within myself—a safe place where fear cannot thrive.

Prayer

Imagine a moment when you're full of uncertainty because fear has taken hold. When life presents challenges that feel unbearable, it's easy to forget the strength that lies within us and that we are not alone. This is when leaning on a higher power becomes essential.

I come from a long line of praying women, raised in a Baptist church where faith was our anchor. I've witnessed my mother pace the floor many nights, immersed in deep prayer with tears streaming down her cheeks, uncertain of how bills would be paid or how to navigate the heartaches she faced. She always turned to God, her higher power. Despite how bad things appeared to be, it always seemed to work out in the end.

I remember my Grandma Rosa stretching out her hands and proclaiming, "Father, I stretch my hands to Thee, no other help I know. If Thou withdraw Thyself from me, whither shall I go?" This bible verse was a beacon of hope and strength for her, as it also is for me.

The greatest wellspring of wisdom, the greatest treasure chest of solutions, resides deep within us. We often look to the outside world for answers, but the magic happens when we look within. Yes, that divine energy lives within us. The very essence of God resides within us, and this divine energy is there, ready to guide us through the scariest battle and stormiest sea. Think of this higher power as your guardian angel, always there in the shadows, whispering gentle words of reassurance and love, and shining a guiding light when you lose your way. Prayer can provide a sense of support and connection, reminding you that you are not alone.

Meditation

Meditation is that sacred space that you cultivate within—a sanctuary for your soul where inner peace flourishes. It invites you to quiet the chaotic noise both inside and around you, allowing you to reconnect with your true essence. In this stillness, meditation becomes the key that unlocks the door to clarity and insight. It offers you the opportunity to explore your fears at their core, illuminating their root causes so that you can confront them with wisdom and grace. As you embark on this journey, you will find the strength to release the hold fear has over you.

I often say that prayer is when you ask God or your higher power for guidance, while meditation is when you sit in quiet anticipation to hear the response. The beauty of meditation is that it can be practiced anywhere. Your car, living room, bathroom—even a cozy closet. The key is to drown out the distractions and immerse yourself in your tranquil space. Personally, I find solace in wordless music, like classical or instrumental gospel tunes or the sound of running water. These help me gather my thoughts and gently drift into that sacred quietude.

Remember, this is your journey. Embrace the freedom to experiment and discover what resonates best with you, allowing your meditation practice to evolve into a true reflection of your inner self.

Positive Affirmations

The power of positive affirmations is amazing. By consciously repeating empowering statements like "Yes I can" you rewire your subconscious mind. The mind believes whatever we tell it, positive or negative. That means fearful thoughts can be replaced with confidence and self-belief. Affirmations are little love notes to yourself, intended to remind you of your inner strength, courage, and limitless potential. I have little sticky pad notes on my bedroom and bathroom walls and mirrors. That way I can see them when I wake up in the morning and before I go to bed at night. I even keep some on my car dashboard when I'm really in a manifesting stage or facing a challenge.

It was in the middle of my marriage chaos that prayer became my lifeline. I was yearning for my own happiness but had a strong desire to shield my family from hurt. It was in these whispered conversations with God that I began to form a resolution. With each quiet moment I spent in prayer and meditation, I began to discern the difference between fear and intuition. You know that gut feeling that tells you when something is good or bad for you? I realized that fear was clouding my judgment, but my intuition—that soft, gentle knowing—is aligned with God's guidance. It was through this connection that I started to see my path clearly. I constantly spoke positive affirmations to myself. "Girl, you can do this." "You deserve happiness." "You are worthy of living a life free from fear and full of joy."

The decision to get a divorce wasn't made in haste. It was a process of unfolding. Leaning on a higher power gave me the courage to acknowledge my own needs and desires, as well as the ability to let go of what no longer served my growth. I felt at peace knowing I was making the right choice.

The dreaded conversation I needed to have with my husband turned out beautiful. He agreed that we should part ways. It was the first time in a long time that we agreed on something without arguing. Our souls found solace in the honesty we shared, and we parted as friends, not enemies. To me this was confirmation that the right choice was made.

Transformation often finds its roots in moments of uncertainty. It is during these times that your dreams are waiting to be birthed, waiting for you to gather the courage to pursue them. This is where your connection to a higher power will shine the brightest. It will be the voice that encourages you to take a step, even when doubt and fear tries to hold you back.

So, Queen, take time to nurture this beautiful connection. Take time out for stillness and reflection in your day. Maybe a heartfelt prayer, a quiet meditation, or simple conversation with your higher power. Don't forget to speak positively to yourself. Be kind and gentle with yourself. It's all about releasing your worries, placing trust in your journey, and allowing the higher power to flow through you.

"Through prayer and meditation, she continues to nurture her inner queen, the one who reigns with wisdom and compassion. Fearlessly steering her life's journey."

Chapter 7

Harnessing Wisdom: The Power of Knowledge

"Knowledge becomes power when put into action."
—author unknown

WELCOME BACK, QUEEN! LET'S TAKE a moment to reflect on our journey so far, particularly that empowering Chapter Five about journaling. Remember how we embraced the symbolism of the pen as our royal scepter and its power? With each stroke of the pen, you begin to gain clarity and perspective. You are not just writing words; you're creating a pathway to healing and growth. You become the ruler of your mental landscape, declaring that you won't let fear dictate your actions any longer.

Well, in this chapter we are going to dive in even deeper. We are raging war against fear! We are going to use knowledge as our sword and impenetrable shield against the fears that dare to cross our path. This is **the fifth powerful step** in breaking free from the chains of fear.

In the early part of Chapter Two, we explored the characteristics of fear, including its powerful ability to emotionally and mentally paralyze us. Fear can cloud our decision making, restrict our exploration of new opportunities, and strip away our self-confidence. Overcoming these fears is essential for both personal and professional growth, and knowledge is a key factor in breaking free from the chains of fear. The truth is, most people are intimidated by the unknown, but when we acquire the knowledge we need, fear begins to lose its grip.

I want you to take a moment to imagine this. Picture your dream. The one that you haven't made a reality yet, but there is this burning desire to. This dream wakes you up at night. It makes you smile when you think about it, but it remains in the One Day Club. Despite the burning passion, two opposing forces battle for control over your mind, positive and negative. We will name the positive Mrs. Yes I Can and the negative Mrs. Defeat.

Now, Mrs. Defeat is very skilled in her craft. She whispers insidious doubts into your ear, planting seeds of self-doubt: *You can't do this. You aren't smart enough. Where are you going to get the money? You're too old. Where are you going to find the time?*

Does this sound familiar?

The beautiful truth in this scenario is that you don't need to have all the pieces figured out just yet. The journey towards your dream must begin somewhere, and it starts with one crucial step. Fire Mrs. Defeat. Replace your doubt with knowledge and nurture your curiosity. Equip yourself with knowledge, the tool that will empower you to translate that burning desire into reality. This will allow Mrs. Yes I Can to take the lead.

Fear is an indication that you are onto something great. When you feel fear rise, it's your call to take action. It's time to pick up your sword and shield of knowledge to win the battle ahead. Flip the script and show fear who the real Queen is. After all, Queens rule!

Knowledge is the lantern that illuminates the paths before you. It's the bridge between where you are and where you want to be. Think of going on a treasure hunt picking up gold and silver coins of wisdom along the way. Every step you take towards understanding brings you closer to your dream. You are no longer limited by the unknown. The pieces of the puzzle are now coming together. There is now a light at the end of the tunnel.

Now, we can't talk about knowledge and leave technology out. Technology is like the wind beneath your wings, a breath of fresh air. It was very difficult to maneuver in the beginning for an older Queen like me, but once I had the youngsters teach me, it became easy and has become my best friend, especially for my business. With just a few clicks, you can access a treasure of knowledge, wisdom, and inspiration that can light up your path like never before. With a simple search, you can connect with experts from all around the world and tap into resources that were once out of reach. The great thing about this is you don't even have to leave your home to gain access to all this knowledge.

Whether your dream is to start a new business, learn a new language, craft or skill, technology offers you the tools to feed your hunger for knowledge. There are online courses, webinars, podcasts, eBooks, and so much more.

Let's talk about the power of being connected. Technology gave us social media, online communities, and networking platforms. You can connect with like-minded people who share your dreams and aspirations. You can find mentors who have walked the path you are on and are more than willing to guide you along the way.

Once you gain knowledge you must use it. It's not something you collect and sit on a shelf. Why learn everything about baking a cake if you're never going to step foot in a kitchen? You'll only miss out on the joy, messiness, and triumph of creating something sweet and delicious to share with others.

As you put your knowledge into practice, something magical unfolds: your confidence begins to grow. It's like planting a little seed. As you nourish it, the seed begins to sprout and eventually will blossom into a beautiful tree. Every move you make, every action you take is like nourishment for that tree. Before you know it, your confidence will be unshakable.

I can't end this chapter without a story to tell. I love teaching with examples. This story is all about how I used knowledge as my sword and shield to become a nurse. I had this burning desire to be a nurse for a very long time. Every time I closed my eyes, I could see myself wearing that nurse's uniform, making a real difference in people's lives. But do you know what happened? Mrs. Defeat kept making her unwelcome visits, whispering doubts in my ear: *Nursing is hard, you will need strong math and science skills, and where are you going to get those? On top of that, it's expensive and time consuming. How can you juggle school, work, and two small children?*

Not only did Mrs. Defeat plague my mind, but she also began to infiltrate my family and friends, planting seeds of doubt in their mind too. They verbally expressed their doubts and concerns to me as well. And to my disbelief, even my own mother joined in with the discouragements. Mrs. Defeat is truly something else.

These concerns were valid, yet they didn't mean I could not pursue my dream. I just needed knowledge and a plan. Instead, I unwittingly welcomed

Mrs. Defeat into my home. Heck, I even invited her to take up space on my metaphorical couch! Slowly, my confidence started to chip away. I found myself doubting my own ability. I felt in my spirit that nursing was my calling, but what if I couldn't succeed? And guess what? I allowed those negative thoughts to win and I put my dream on the shelf.

One day I had a wake-up call. I realized that these doubts were costing me more than I could imagine—my happiness, my dreams, financial stability, and a better life for my children. In that moment, I decided, no more playing it small, no more listening to the naysayers. Mrs. Defeat had to go! It was time for me to go after my dream with every fiber of my being. That day me and Mrs. Yes I Can became best friends. I became a nurse in my mind, heart, and soul. I just needed professional training. It was like a switch had flipped within me. I was determined to make my dream a reality.

But here is where the magic of knowledge comes in. The first thing I did was learn to move in silence. It was the best thing I ever did. This is a very important step. People can't give you opinions on what they don't know about. I secretly enrolled in Nursing School. I told no one except my mother in the early stages.

Then I took a deep dive into everything nursing. I researched, I read. This was thirty years ago. Technology wasn't as advanced as it is today. I surrounded myself with nurses, soaking up their stories and wisdom. I asked them lots of questions. Did it completely erase my fears? No, it didn't, but something incredible happened. With every ounce of knowledge I gained, the fear took a step back. You see, I gained something so valuable—a roadmap to follow. It was like shining a light into a dark room. Suddenly, those shadows on the walls weren't so scary anymore. I wasn't just arming myself with facts; I was building a fortress of understanding.

And oh, those nurses I surrounded myself with became my mentors and guides on my journey. It was like having allies of surrounding nations there to help me just in case fear threatened war again. They would come onto the battlefield with me to help with whatever I needed. Whether it was studying, helping me to write papers, or even babysitting.

So, I didn't become a nurse just by enrolling in nursing school and putting on that uniform. No, my friend. I became a nurse when I made the choice to seek knowledge, when I decided that fear was a steppingstone and not a roadblock.

You want to know the most beautiful part of the story? I became more than a nurse. I became the healer, the caregiver, the leader, and the light-bearer I was always destined to be. My family, once hesitant, became my biggest cheerleaders when they saw me forging my path toward fulfilling my dream. My mother emerged as my proudest and most devoted supporter. The day I walked across the stage as a student government President with 3.98 GPA and multiple student achievement awards, I handed my Certificate of Nursing to her. She'd earned it just as much as I had.

So, my radiant Queen, as we come to the end of this captivating chapter, remember that knowledge isn't just power. It's your beacon of light, your sword, your shield, and your fortress. Seek, learn, and soar. Know that you possess the tools to rewrite your narrative, relinquishing uncertainty while reigning supreme over your fears. The journey ahead promises to be nothing short of inspiring, and in the next chapter, we will learn how to take baby steps, so it doesn't feel overwhelming.

Chapter 8
Embracing the Dance of Baby Steps

"Don't let the entire staircase overwhelm you. Just focus on that first step."

—author unknown

WELCOME BACK! WOW! TIME IS moving quickly. We are already on **the sixth powerful step** to breaking free from the chains of fear. I hope you are finding this information helpful so far.

Now, we've already discussed how fear has a way of making our goals seem out of reach. It can prevent us from taking the necessary steps to proceed, especially when we allow ourselves to become overwhelmed with all the steps needed to reach our goal. It's like standing at the shoreline looking out at a beautiful island—your dream destination—but you are unsure how to get there.

The beautiful island represents your hopes and aspirations. However, the large body of water between you and the island symbolizes the fear and uncertainty you feel. You have no idea how deep the water is, the potential challenges you may face, or any idea of the actual distance. This can make the journey seem overwhelming.

Now, let me ask you—have you ever had a dream or goal that seemed so grand, so ambitious, that the mere thought of the effort required to achieve it caused you to freeze in your tracks? It is a very common experience, one that can deter us from pursuing our dreams. This is where the magic of baby steps comes in. You see, no matter the journey, short or long, it all starts with one step.

When I wanted to create my first business, I was so excited that I jumped straight into naming the service and figuring out the skillset needed to provide it. However, I quickly became overwhelmed by all the aspects to consider, and I stopped. I focused too much on the end results and everything I believed was required to get there instead of taking it step by step. I allowed people who had never accomplished what I was aiming for to get into my head, and the weight of their doubts contributed to my paralysis. This was supposed to be a joyous time, but it quickly turned into a nightmare. So, I quit, and a year would pass before I revisited the idea.

At times, we allow the enormity of the staircase to intimidate us. We become afraid of its steepness and how many steps there are. We become so consumed with the top of the staircase that we lose sight of the importance of the first step. Instead of focusing on the entire journey, we should concentrate on taking one step at a time. We also should stop worrying about making mistakes. In life there are no mistakes, only lessons. Each fumble or misstep is not a mark of failure. It is an opportunity for growth. Every challenge we face, every obstacle we overcome, teaches us something new and valuable, shaping us into wiser and stronger individuals. So don't let mistakes scare you. Instead, embrace them, learn from them, and let them guide you on your journey towards your dreams.

Let's take a moment to reflect on the amazing wisdom of children and how we can apply their tactics to overcome our own fears and doubts.

Babies don't start off running. First, they crawl. Then they become more adventurous by learning how to pull themselves up, using furniture as their trusty aid. Then the magic begins. Slowly, they dare to take the first step. It may be wobbly, they may stumble and fall, but they don't let it stop them. They rise and try again, more determined than the last time. There may be tears, moments of frustration, even temper tantrums. Sometimes they may hurt themselves trying to master the art of walking. However, they persist. One step follows another, each one building their confidence until suddenly they are off and running. Children aren't afraid of making mistakes. They understand these are steppingstones to something bigger and better.

Babies are also masters of adaptability. Despite their age, children have the innate ability to tweak their game plan in order to figure things out and get what they want. They'll try again and again, searching for solutions to put a toy together, how to get something out of reach or get themselves out of a confined area. When the going gets tough they have the wisdom to ask for help.

I remember observing my son when he was just two years old. He was determined to get a box of cereal from the top of the refrigerator. He had no idea I was watching him, but I saw him push a chair from the kitchen table over to the refrigerator. He climbed up on the chair, then up onto the countertop, all to reach this elusive cereal box.

When he realized he was still too short, he climbed back down, opened a drawer and strategically chose a long-handled spoon. Climbing back up on the chair and then onto the countertop, he knocked the cereal box over, finally managing to reach it. The joy on his face when he accomplished his goal was priceless! Yet, when he couldn't open the brand-new box, he ran to me for help. He understood that, while he had achieved what he had set out to do—which was to get the box of cereal—he still needed help with his next step, which was to open it. He wasn't ashamed to ask for help, even knowing he was not supposed to have the cereal. I could not say no after he went through all that trouble.

Then there comes a time when fear and doubt creep in, whispering in their innocent ears. Parents, society, and even religion sometimes tell them what they can't do and what they should fear. They quickly lose that innate ability to just go for what they want, in exchange for needing approval and reassurance to try.

Applying the Baby Steps Principle to Fear:

1. **Recognize Your Fear:** Just as a baby acknowledges the need to learn to walk, you must first recognize your fear. Understand what's holding you back and name it.

2. **Comfort Zone Stretching:** Pushing yourself slightly beyond your comfort level is essential for growth, but it's important to do so in a way that doesn't trigger overwhelming fear. By gradually exposing ourselves to what makes us uncomfortable, we can build confidence and silence.

3. **Setting Smaller Goals:** Babies don't try to run before they can even stand. They usually crawl first. Set small, attainable goals for yourself that push your boundaries. These small victories will build your confidence and reduce fear.

4. **Learning from Each Step:** Babies stumble and fall when they learn to walk. So, expect setbacks and missteps in your journey. Learn from them and use them as steppingstones.

5. **The Patience of Baby Steps:** Babies don't rush their progress, and neither should you. Take

your time but persistently move forward step by step. Be gentle and kind with yourself. Celebrate each small victory along the way. Most of all, don't be afraid to ask for help.

Embracing baby steps was essential when I decided to launch my coaching business. It felt downright crazy to switch careers in my fifties, especially after a successful nursing career where I was well-versed in my craft. Coaching? That was a whole new ballgame! However, it had become my passion, and I believe once you conquer one challenge in life, you're equipped to conquer many more.

So, I acknowledged the fear and took a hard look at the root cause. Armed with the power of the pen, I embraced the harmonious Trinity of Empowerment. By using knowledge as my sword and impenetrable shield, I was able to embrace the baby steps. Here I am today, a transformational life coach, speaker, and published author.

As you begin to take these small, manageable steps, you'll notice something incredible. *Progress.* The power of progress will help your confidence to grow and your fear to shrink. What you once thought was insurmountable is now another challenge conquered.

Now, don't go away. We are going to learn how to paint your path to success in the next chapter. See you there!

Chapter 9
Paint Your Path to Success: The Power of Visualization

"Visualize this thing that you want, see it, feel it, believe in it. Make your mental blueprint and begin to build!"

—Robert Collier

WELCOME TO **THE SEVENTH POWERFUL step** on your journey to breaking free from the chains of fear. In the previous chapter, we explored the idea of breaking your goals into smaller, manageable pieces. This simple yet powerful approach not only makes your goals more achievable but also helps you to see progress quickly. As a result, your confidence grows and your fear shrinks. To see your accomplishments begin to thrive will fill you with eagerness, motivating you to continue pursuing your goals more enthused than ever.

In this chapter we'll explore a powerful tool that will not only calm your fear but also guide you toward your dreams with unwavering confidence. Visualization is the art of bringing your mental images to life. It's the process of turning your thoughts into reality.

Queen, I want you to think of yourself as an artist and your mind as your royal paint brush. With the boundless power of your imagination, you can design your own destiny. I need you to understand how powerful your imagination is. It simply gives you previews of life's coming attractions. Everything begins on the inside before it is seen on the outside. Everything ever invented was first a picture painted in someone's mind. They could see it completed before they started to build it. An architect draws out the plans of a building before one brick is laid. A writer envisions the conclusion of the story before crafting its beginning and middle.

Visualization isn't just daydreaming. It is a practice that ignites your confidence. It's like rehearsing success in your mind. When you can picture every step of an event or everything going exactly as you want, you prepare your mind and body to take those steps in real life.

As I was nearing the completion of nursing school, my next goal was to move my children and myself out of New York. I was living in public housing in Brooklyn and craved to break this cycle. I knew that gaining experience as a nurse and saving money were crucial steps towards accomplishing this goal. I understood that it would take some time to do this. I set a goal for two years.

I was so excited that I talked about it often. However, some of my childhood friends couldn't grasp my vision. They often teased me for talking about moving so much. "You've been talking about this for ages, and you're still right here with us," they'd say. Their words hurt very badly. I decided at that very moment to once again move in silence. I also started distancing myself from them. I was no better than them. After all, we all have dreams. I just had a current plan of action for mine. I was on a mission to get out and I didn't need negativity in my life trying to hold me back.

I made a promise to them and myself on that day, that I would not bring up moving again. They would know I was leaving when a green and yellow Mayflower moving truck showed up and I walked outside to greet the driver. Queen, I want you to remember this statement.

During those silent days, I used my royal brush to paint a picture in my mind. I could see the joy and feel the pride and sense of accomplishment that would wash over me when the day finally arrived. Fear tried to creep in every now and then. After all, moving to a new state far away from my family as a single mom was a big leap. However, I knew deep inside that it was the best choice for my children and me. I leaned on the Trinity of Empowerment to get me through. Journaling my thoughts, praying for guidance, and using positive affirmations.

Every single day and night, I revisited that mental image. Now, I want you to understand this move didn't magically happen. I had to take massive action. I researched what was needed to make this move possible. I worked my butt off. I saved more money than I ever thought possible. I flew to South Carolina for a few days to look at houses and apartments and get a better idea of where I would live. I visited the schools my children would attend. I went to the grocery stores, the shopping malls, parks, and roller-skating rinks. This made it feel more real. I could see my family living there. I even recorded the sound of a rooster crowing in the morning, so I could listen to it when I returned home.

My trip to South Carolina helped me visualize my dream of moving in a more tangible way. Visiting potential apartments and schools for my children allowed me to see what this new life could look like. It gave me a clear idea to work toward and made the dream feel real.

I was so happy and became more confident as I began knocking out my baby steps. Each step brought me closer to my dream. This is where the magic happened. Everything I needed started gravitating toward me, aligning perfectly with my vision. I knew I was onto something when I was able to purchase my car with cash in preparation for the move. In the end, it only took one year and three months to achieve my goal, instead of the two years I had allotted myself.

Fast forward to when the day I'd been visualizing finally arrived. That green and yellow Mayflower truck, the symbol of my achievement, pulled up. What's even more incredible is that those same friends who teased me were sitting on the bench in front of my apartment building, just as I had imagined when I walked out to greet the driver. This is a testament to how potent your thoughts and words are. I still use this tool today. I visualized this book long before I wrote it.

Visualization, my Queen, is a powerful tool. It's about seeing, feeling, and living your dreams in your mind before they become reality. Have you ever tried it? Have you ever envisioned something you desired so vividly that you could almost touch it, even before it happened?

Let's talk about the science behind visualization. When you visualize your success, your brain can't tell the difference between what's real and what's imagined. It releases feel-good chemicals like dopamine and serotonin, making you feel happy and motivated. This positivity not only boosts your confidence but also helps to fight fear and anxiety.

How to Start Visualizing Your Success:

1. **Give Yourself Permission To Dream:** Often we don't allow ourselves to dream or plan big. We limit ourselves because of the negative things we're told, we have our own self-limiting beliefs, or we let our past determine our future. You must believe that you are worthy and deserving of that thing you want.

2. **Define Your Goals:** Clearly define what it is you want to do. Is it starting a business, traveling the world, going back to school, or achieving a particular milestone in your career? Be very specific.

3. **Research What It Will Take:** Research what you will need to bring it to fruition. Write it down, just like you would write the ingredients down in order to bake a cake. Set a reasonable deadline for completion. Make room for mishaps or setbacks.

4. **Create Your Sanctuary:** This should be a quiet space where you won't be disturbed. It can be at home, in your car, or at a park. Sit down

and close your eyes, take a few breaths in, and slowly exhale. Let go of the outside world for a few moments.

5. **Start Visualizing Your Dream:** Engage all your senses. What do you see, hear, smell, taste, and touch in your vision of success? Now, use your royal paint brush to paint those beautiful colors of success in your mind. You must see yourself taking those steps needed to make your goal or dream a reality. You need to see and feel yourself doing the work. You must imagine the emotions you'll experience when you accomplish each step. Every step should be designed to help you achieve your goals. Feel pride, joy, and confidence in your heart. Let those feelings wash over you.

6. **Take Massive Action:** Nothing is going to happen if you don't act. Even to win the lottery you must buy a ticket. Take baby steps and start checking off the list of ingredients one by one. With determination and hard work, you will see that dream or goal become a reality.

7. **Revisit Daily:** Visualization takes practice; it is not a one-time event. Make it part of your daily routine. When you wake up and before you go

to bed, take a few minutes to paint your path to success.

As you paint your path to success through visualization, you are rewiring your brain. Fear begins to lose its grip because you've already experienced the success of what you want in your mind. Your confidence grows, and you become more resilient to the challenges that lie ahead.

So, Queen, I invite you to pick up your royal paint brush, dip it into the colors of your dreams, and start painting your path to success. The more vivid and real you make it in your mind, the more unstoppable you will become. Remember, you are the artist of your destiny, and with the power of visualization, you can overcome fear and conquer the world.

Make sure you don't ditch the final chapter. I have some important information about the reality of pursuing your goals.

Chapter 10

The Power of Influence: Surround Yourself with Successful People

"Hang around successful people. People who inspire and inform you. Find role models, not roadblocks."

—Jeffrey Gitomer

WELCOME BACK BEAUTIFUL QUEEN. I can't believe we are already in the final chapter and **step eight** of breaking free from the chains of fear. In the previous chapter, we delved into the incredible power of visualization in painting a vibrant path towards success. However, my friend, embarking on this journey can sometimes feel lonely. It's not easy. That's why in this chapter I want to emphasize the significance of surrounding yourself with people who not only dream big but also take bold action to transform those dreams into tangible realities. I refer to these extraordinary people as "Dreamers and Doers."

We've already discussed how fear often stems from the unknown, from the uncertainty of whether you can truly achieve your dreams. However, when you are in the presence of those who've already walked the path of success, fear loosens its grip. Their stories of triumph become a warm and comforting light, gently illuminating the way forward, guiding you towards your own dreams and aspirations.

Your dreams are a precious treasure, a vision that ignites your soul with passion and purpose. However, not everyone will fully grasp or support your aspirations. In your excitement and enthusiasm, you might find yourself sharing your dreams openly, only to encounter smirks and negative comments from others. Do you remember my story about moving from New York City to South Carolina? My friends at the time shut me down when I spoke about my dreams.

Your excitement, though meant to be an inspiration, can sometimes be misconstrued as bragging or bothersome to those who have yet to witness your dreams manifest. Jealousy and envy may arise because you are actively taking steps to ensure the reality of your dreams, while others may have dreams without a concrete plan. It's essential to be discerning about who you confide in to protect the sanctity of your vision and your emotional wellbeing.

In life, the company we keep can make all the difference. Have you heard the old saying "birds of a feather flock together"? It's an old proverb that means people with the same interest and taste will usually be found socializing together. Have you ever watched a flock of birds in the sky? They lift each other up, ride the currents together, and reach new heights as a collective. Similarly, the people you surround yourself with can either hold you back or propel you toward your dreams. I call my flock my "soul tribe." One outing or phone call with this amazing group of women makes me feel so powerful and courageous. I can show my weakness and vulnerability with them, without the fear of being judged or criticized. They hold me accountable to my goals, keeping me on my path, even when fear tries to divert me.

Your environment and the people you choose to be around are potent influences on your mindset, your choices, and ultimately, your destiny. When you surround yourself with successful individuals, you're immersing yourself in a culture of achievement. Successful people possess a unique energy—they radiate confidence, determination, and resilience. When you're around them, you naturally absorb these qualities. It's like osmosis. Your mindset begins to shift, and you start to believe that success is not only attainable but also within your reach.

In contrast, remember in Chapter 4, I experienced a similar effect with my mother's fear of driving. Growing up around her anxiousness, I gradually absorbed that fear, thinking it was part of me. Just as I would soak up the positive attributes of successful people, the anxiety I witnessed in my mother became my own. This comparison highlights the power of our surroundings, showing that both fear and success can shape our beliefs and behaviors, depending on who we spend time with.

The amazing thing about surrounding yourself with successful people is that you're not just gaining mentors and role models. You are also expanding your network. You will have access to opportunities, valuable insights, and connections that can open doors you never thought possible.

Actively seek opportunities to connect with successful individuals. Embrace learning. Attend networking events, seminars, or workshops related to your goals. Don't be afraid to approach successful people for mentorship. Many will be delighted by your interest and are more than willing to share their wisdom and guide others on their journey.

Remember, success is a two-way street. Offer your support, wisdom, and encouragement to others on their journey. You don't have to wait until you achieve ultimate success to help others. Even if you're not an expert in every area, you have valuable skills to share. For instance, if you're savvy with computer skills, you can assist not only your colleagues but also a mentor who is not proficient in technology. Your insights can benefit them and your generosity will strengthen your network but also enhance your own growth and self-confidence.

Queen, it is crucial to maintain persistence and be resilient on your path to success. Along this journey, you are bound to face setbacks and moments of fear that may test your determination. However, it is during these challenging times that you can rely on your invaluable network for guidance and motivation.

Take a moment to assess the people you spend the most time with. Do they uplift and inspire you, or do they bring negativity and doubt into your life?

Choose the people you confide in wisely. Limit your time with individuals who possess dreams without a plan. Do this not out of unkindness, but because their lack of direction might inadvertently pull you away from your own path. Their uncertain energy can be like a fog obstructing the clarity of your vision and impeding the flow of positive energy towards your goals.

That's it, Queen! If you aspire to be successful at anything in life and wish to diminish the grip of fear, remember that your environment matters. Surround yourself with dreamers and achievers. A network of successful people will transform your solo journey into a group-empowering expedition.

Together with your own soul tribe, you can conquer fear and breathe life into your boldest dreams!

Conclusion

"I learned that courage was not the absence of fear, but the triumph over it. The brave man is not he who does not feel afraid, but he who conquers that fear."

—Nelson Mandela

Okay, beautiful Queen. We are here at the end of our journey together. Let's take a moment to reflect on the valuable lessons we've uncovered in **the eight powerful steps** that will equip you to face your fears head-on and continue to move forward.

Step 1: Acknowledge Your Fears

You've learned that it's perfectly normal to be afraid at times. Acknowledging your fears is the first step toward conquering them.

Step 2: Identify the Root Cause

Dig deep to unearth the origins of your fears. Understanding where they stem from empowers you to confront and dismantle them with poise and grace.

Step 3: Journal About Your Fear

Your journal is your confidante, a sacred space into which you pour out your heart and soul. The act of putting your fears into words will allow you to gain clarity and perspective, transforming your fears into manageable challenges.

Step 4:
The Power of Prayer, Meditation, and Positive Affirmations

Through prayer, meditation, and the repetition of positive affirmations, you will tap into a higher power and the wellspring of your inner strength. These practices will nurture your spirit, guiding you through moments of uncertainty and doubt.

Step 5:
Knowledge is Power

Education will be your ally on your journey. Seek knowledge relentlessly. Recognize it is the key to unlocking new opportunities and dismantling the walls that fear constructs. Don't be afraid to monetarily invest in yourself. You are worth it!

Step 6:
Take Small Steps

Embrace the power of taking small, deliberate steps towards your goals. Each step, no matter how small, will move you closer to your dreams, proving that progress is the antidote to fear.

Step 7:
Visualization

Through the art of visualization, you can materialize your dreams before your very eyes. You can cultivate the ability to see success even in the face of adversity, knowing that your mind shapes your reality.

Step 8:
Surround Yourself with Successful People

It is important to surround yourself with the radiant light of success. Your soul tribe will remind you of your innate potential. They will encourage, mentor, and guide you on your journey to success.

Conclusion

Queen, as we come to the close of this journey together, I want you to hold onto one important truth. Fear is not your enemy. It is your friend in disguise because it serves as a catalyst for growth and transformation. Don't allow it to confine you. Instead, harness its energy to propel yourself toward your goals and desires.

So, when you feel scared, remember to do it anyway. You now have the tools you need to embrace your fear, take those steps, and continue to reign over your destiny with grace and strength. The path ahead is bright, and you are ready to walk it with confidence and determination. The world awaits your brilliance, your passion, and your unique imprint.

Enclosing I want to share this quote that I absolutely adore by an American author, Neale Donald Walsch:

"Life begins at the end of your comfort zone."

It means that It is beyond your fear and uncertainties that you find your true potential and the most beautiful, fulfilling experiences. It's time to take that leap, my courageous Queen, and start living your best life. Whatever that looks like to you.

I sincerely hope you have enjoyed this book and discovered the power of these eight powerful steps as much as I have cherished sharing them with you. If this book has touched your heart, consider gifting it to someone who might need it. Often, we give others what they want instead of what they truly need.

Thank you for spending your valuable time with me and allowing me to be your guide on this journey. I miss you already. Wishing you peace, happiness, and success in all your endeavors, and sending much love.

Bye for now, but not for long, as my next book, *The Eight Pillars to Self-Love*: The Master Key to Life, will be arriving soon!

Queen

About the Author

MEET SANDRA, AFFECTIONATELY KNOWN AS a spirited and compassionate individual with an unwavering passion for life and a genuine love for people. With a mission to inspire and empower others, Sandra is dedicated to helping individuals unlock their true potential and become the best versions of themselves.

An adventurous soul, she has traveled to 70 countries solo, immersing herself in diverse cultures and enriching her life with their rich histories. It was on these solo adventures that Sandra gained a deep spiritual connection and found the true meaning of self-love.

This, lead her to publish her first book, "On My Own: A Guide to Finding Yourself through Female Solo Travel." Alongside her travels, Sandra enjoys blogging, crafting exquisite jewelry, exploring various music genres, designing captivating book journal covers and most of all spending time with her family.

For the past three decades, she has devoted herself to nursing as an emergency room trauma nurse, spending the last 15 years in nursing leadership as a Nurse Administrator. Now, she embarks on an exciting new chapter as a Transformational Life Coach and Speaker. Her expertise encompasses self-love, leadership, and chakra healing, shaped by her personal journey through self-doubt, low self-esteem, and fear.

Through her transformative practices, Sandra empowers women to harness their internal power, helping them navigate the obstacles that stand in the way of their dreams. With her unique blend of experience and compassion, she guides her clients to achieve their aspirations and lead lives filled with purpose, fulfillment, and prosperity.

About the Author

Sandra is a dynamic speaker and orator with an amazing life story and the ability to touch people's hearts and souls.

Join Sandra on this inspiring journey, and remember: So, what you are scared, girl, do it anyway!

Keep In Touch

Instagram @coachingwithqueen
Facebook @Sandra Gemini-Queen Parker
LinkedIn @Sandra (Queen) Parker
Email: Sandra@coachingwithqueen.com

To Get Your Free Intro to
Self Love Guide Today

On My Own A Guide to Solo Travel

To Order Your Copy Today

www.ingramcontent.com/pod-product-compliance
Lightning Source LLC
Chambersburg PA
CBHW070118080526
44586CB00013B/1332